OPENING THE HOLY DOOR

"What the holy doors of St. Peter's Basilica do every quarter century, Joan Watson enables the reader to do any day of the year: enter the mysteries of salvation history, connect personally with them, and walk from woundedness and loss to hope. Watson opens the door to a unique journey through salvation history. Combining sacred art and scripture reflection, she draws the reader into the mysteries of our faith, makes connections to life today, and helps us walk the path from woundedness and loss to freedom and hope. I highly recommend *Opening the Holy Door* for individual or group reflection."

Sarah Christmyer
Bible teacher and author of *Becoming Women of the Word*

"Joan Watson arrives just in time to help us make the most of the Jubilee Year, a grace created especially for you and me and our generation. God wants us to understand this grace and correspond to it. He wants us to bring our family and friends along with us. This book shows us how. This book is powerful."

Mike Aquilina
Author and editor of the Reclaiming Catholic History series

"When Joan Watson offers spiritual wisdom, I pay attention. You should too. *Opening the Holy Door* has already deepened my hope in Jesus—and it will do the same for you."

J. D. Flynn
Editor-in-Chief of The Pillar

"What barriers do we need to break through? What defenses do we need to drop? What do we need to unlock to fully embrace the wonder, mercy, and hope of God's love? This Holy Year is a perfect opportunity to explore those questions, and this heart-stopping book is the perfect companion for the journey."

From the foreword by Deacon Greg Kandra
Author of *A Deacon Prays* and *Befriending St. Joseph*

OPENING THE HOLY DOOR

Hope-Filled Scripture Reflections from St. Peter's Basilica

JOAN WATSON

Ave Maria Press AVE Notre Dame, Indiana

Nihil Obstat: Reverend Monsignor Michael Heintz, PhD
          Censor Librorum
Imprimatur: Most Reverend Kevin C. Rhoades
          Bishop of Fort Wayne–South Bend
          Given at Fort Wayne, Indiana, on 13 August 2024

The *Nihil Obstat* and *Imprimatur* are official declarations that a book or pamphlet is free of doctrinal or moral error. No implication is contained therein that those who have granted the *Nihil Obstat* or *Imprimatur* agree with its contents, opinions, or statements expressed.

Foreword © 2024 by Greg Kandra

Founded in 1865, Ave Maria Press is a ministry of the United States Province of Holy Cross.

www.avemariapress.com

Paperback: ISBN-13 978-1-64680-387-3

E-book: ISBN-13 978-1-64680-388-0

Cover image © Associated Press.

Image of Holy Door © Fczarnowski via Wikimedia Commons.

Image of Holy Door panels © www.stpetersbasilica.info. Used with permission.

Cover and text design by Andy Wagoner.

Printed and bound in the United States of America.

Library of Congress Cataloging-in-Publication Data is available.

To Larry Pryor, my Barnabas,
who believed in my Bible studies enough to
put them on paper
1968–2020

Contents

Foreword by Deacon Greg Kandra   ix

Author's Note: About the Holy Door   xii
of St. Peter's Basilica

Introduction: When Hope Is Lost   2

1. A Promise Fulfilled   8

2. He Leads, We Follow   18

3. What Really Binds Us   24

4. A Father's Heart   32

5. The Necessity of Love   40

6. The High Cost of Mercy   48

7. Hope in the Face of Sin   56

8. Until the End   64

9. The Hope of Being Found   70

10. Poured into Our Hearts   78

11. The Only Man-Made Thing in Heaven   84

12. Go and Do Likewise   92

Conclusion: Moving Forward in Hope   98

Notes   103

Foreword

Honestly, I never even noticed.

During the last Jubilee Year, in 2000, as my wife and I passed through the Holy Door of St. Peter's Basilica and entered that breathtaking nave, our eyes traveled ahead and above, taking in the spectacular play of light, color, shape, and size. Art, history, piety, faith—it was all there. I don't remember if my jaw was hanging open, but it probably was. I was setting foot in one of the most famous, breathtaking religious spaces in the world. There was so much to take in.

And I never thought to pay attention to the door.

This book you now have before you reminds me of what I missed, and it serves as an inspiring glimpse at what I absolutely *cannot* miss when I make this same journey in 2025. *Pay attention*, it says. There is so much more to see.

Joan Watson has noticed what so many of us don't, and with this slender volume she invites us to see the familiar with new eyes and to pray our way through this Holy Year with a new heart.

Not only that, she is giving new meaning and purpose to the very idea of a door.

Scripture famously tells us "knock and it shall be opened" (Mt 7:7–8) and "I stand at the door and knock" (Rv 3:20). We tend to think of the door as a barrier that needs to be removed, or a gate that needs to be opened, to reveal a yearned-for destination on the other side. (Certainly that's how I felt entering St. Peter's!) But no, there is so much more.

In this book, we are invited to stop, pause, pray, reflect, and dream—to look more closely at the door we are passing through and absorb the stories it tells. At the door, we encounter the full range of salvation history and human experience from heartbreak to hope. Passing through this gateway is more than just a formality or something we have to get through to reach a destination.

It is our story, yours and mine. So it is with every door in life.

What barriers do we need to break through? What defenses do we need to drop? What do we need to unlock to fully embrace the wonder, mercy, and hope of God's love?

This Holy Year is a perfect opportunity to explore those questions, and this door-breaking, heart-stopping book is the perfect companion for the journey.

A familiar saying tells us that when God closes a door, he opens a window. No one ever mentions what happens when he opens a door and invites us in. Consider this year a chance to accept an invitation to grace and to ponder what God has in store. It's a rare moment to step across the threshold and accept possibility. Prepare to be transformed.

But first, stop, pause, look, and wonder. Like so much in life, the very door we walk through has much to tell us, if only we take the time to notice.

Deacon Greg Kandra

Author of *A Deacon Prays* and *Befriending St. Joseph*

About the Holy Door of St. Peter's Basilica

I have been to St. Peter's Basilica more times than I can count. I've gone for early-morning visits alone, led groups of pilgrims on tours, joined large joyful events like Easter Vigil, and attended somber moments like paying respect to both Pope John Paul II and Pope Benedict XVI as they lay in state. I have entered the basilica from its side doors hidden in plain sight, descended from the roof, and emerged from the narrow steps that come from the crypt. But there is one doorway I have never passed through. I have never walked through the Holy Door.

This door is unlike any other entrance to the basilica. It stands as a main entrance, one of the five that lead from the atrium into the main body of the church. But it remains closed, bricked up from the inside. This door is only open during Jubilees, special times of grace that typically occur every twenty-five years. The pope himself opens this Holy Door on Christmas Eve to begin the Jubilee, and graces are given to pilgrims who enter the basilica through this door as a sign of repentance and hope. While behind the door is a simple wall, which must be dismantled by stonemasons prior to the Holy Father's ritual action, the front of the door is beautifully ornate.

As you stand in front of the closed door, its sixteen bronze images take you through salvation history, from an angel expelling the first Eve to an angel greeting the New Eve, through the public ministry of Christ to his Passion and Resurrection. Fittingly, the final panel depicts the Holy Father at the door itself, with the message "I stand at the door and knock." Because, while the door is usually closed to pilgrims, the scenes on the door are a reminder that Jesus Christ, the Gate and the Way, has gone before us to open the door of grace.

This book consists of twelve reflections, each based on a panel of this Holy Door. Each of the twelve panels chosen for meditation depicts a New Testament event or parable that leads us into a deeper understanding of the hope we have in Christ. Before we begin, we'll set the stage as the door does: by asking why the world seems so hopeless. By the end of our time together, I hope you leave with an answer to the question "What now?"

For each of the twelve meditations, I invite you to enter into the New Testament passage in two ways. First, we will **Look with Hope**, exploring each passage through what we could call *visio divina*. This practice is based on the practice of lectio divina, which is a slow, careful reading of the scriptures. Before reading the passage, I encourage you to spend some time looking at a particular panel of the Holy Door. Before reading what I say about the panel, look at the scene and the details the artist chose to depict. Ask questions, let the piece of art draw you into the scene, and stay with the images for a while. Don't rush. Then, when you are ready, I will lead you to think about certain details of the panel.

Second, we will approach the same scene through an Ignatian reading of sacred scripture. Choose your favorite translation of the Bible as your necessary companion to this book. In each chapter, I will invite you to **Turn to the Word**. As you read the passage indicated, place yourself into the scene. Try to read the story or parable as if you have never heard it before, and picture it unfolding around you as you read. What do you see? What do you hear? What do you smell or feel? Use your senses to bring what might be a familiar story to new life. Afterward, we will take what we learned from both of these exercises to see what words of hope God wants to speak through this particular encounter.

This book is suitable for personal or group use. If used in a group, participants could take turns reading the chapter out loud. When it is time to Turn to the Word, the participants could choose to close their eyes and listen to the Word read out loud to more fully enter into the story.

A Word about the Jubilee

The Year of Jubilee, a celebration of the love and mercy of God that occurs every twenty-five years, has origins that can be traced to the Old Testament. In Leviticus 25, God commanded the Israelites to observe a "sabbatical year" every seventh year. It was a year without sowing or reaping, when even the land was given rest. After the seventh sabbatical year, the fiftieth year would be called a Jubilee, a year of celebration and rest dedicated to the Lord. Debts were forgiven, slaves freed, and property returned. One of the greatest examples of social and communal mercy in the Old Testament, the Jubilee allowed the people to learn mercy by giving mercy.

This year of restoration was a physical reminder of the even greater work God wanted to do for his people. In Isaiah 61, the prophet tells Israel that God is going to release them from their slavery and debt. At the beginning of his public ministry, Jesus quotes this prophecy to announce his mission (see Luke 4:18–19). As in all things, Jesus comes not only to fulfill the Old Testament but also to go beyond. He is fulfilling the Old Testament Year of Jubilee, but with a promise of greater restoration: freedom from death and sin.

In 1299, when times were hard due to the effects of plague, war, and material hardship, thousands of Christians eager to amend their lives and seek God's blessing made a pilgrimage to Rome, asking for God's blessing and the protection of the apostles. At that time, it wasn't easy to travel to Rome, and Pope Boniface VIII was so inspired by their faith that he declared 1300 a "year of forgiveness for all sins." Special graces were attached to visiting the tombs of St. Peter and St. Paul. Thus began the tradition of Jubilee years: at first every one hundred years, then fifty, now twenty-five.

One of the hallmarks of the Jubilee year is the opening of each Holy Door of the four major basilicas in Rome: St. John Lateran, St. Paul Outside the Walls, St. Mary Major, and St. Peter. These four doors are opened only during Years of Jubilee, so that pilgrims may pass through them and receive a plenary indulgence for their sins.

Then and now, the Christian Jubilee year has become a time to enter into freedom. It is a time for reconciliation with God and neighbor. As we receive the graces of this year, also called a "Holy Year," we are called to a holiness of life, engaging in acts of mercy and conversion. While we cannot take a break from our "sowing" or "harvesting" for a year, we can find ways to dedicate this year in a special way to the Lord.

While the Jubilee years are profound and unique times in the Church's history, and the Holy Door of St. Peter's Basilica remains open for only a short time, the bronze panels of this door are always visible to pilgrims, mutely testifying to the hope of Christ. Whether or not you join the millions who have and will walk through this door, and whether or not you pick this study up during a Jubilee, my prayer for you is that you allow these images—and the Word of God to which they point—to renew your hope, nourish your faith, and lead you to encounter the living God.

It is Christ who is the true "Holy Door"; it is
he who makes it possible for us to enter the
Father's house and who introduces us into the
intimacy of the divine life.

—Pope John Paul II (January 6, 2001)

When Hope Is Lost

W e need no proof that we live in a broken world. There is no need to present evidence; the case is closed before it is opened. The effects of original sin are apparent in our personal lives as much as they are visible in the world at large.

The third chapter of Genesis tells the sorry tale: that we once had everything, and we threw it away. Sin entered the world . . . and now we live with the wounds.

And yet, that same chapter of Genesis also gives us reason to hope. The world has been damaged, but it is not destroyed. Humankind is wounded and weakened but not lost forever.

It is not by accident that we begin looking at this Holy Door with a discussion of closed doors. The first panels on the door depict the angel set at the gates of paradise, closing the garden and evicting Adam and Eve. Closed doors, the banishment of our first parents. How is this a sign of hope?

Genesis tells us that God closed the garden to Adam and Eve so that they would not eat of the tree of life. For our sake, not his, God explains, "lest [Adam] put forth his hand and take also of the tree of life, and eat, and live for ever" (Gn 3:22).

Contrary to how this might read, those are not the words of a vengeful God who cuts his creation off from eternal life out of anger. Those are the words of a loving God who protects his creation from a life of eternal separation from him. The cherubim and its flaming sword are not punishments but protections. Given Adam and Eve's current state, if they were now to eat of the tree of life, eternity would be hell.

These gates are closed out of love.

And thus, we dare to hope. We dare to hope that this same God who desires not the death of the sinner will also do something to open those gates when they will mean not death but life. And that third chapter of Genesis gives us every reason to hope that will indeed happen.

When hope is lost by the eating of the fruit, the disobedience of our first parents, and the closing of the doors of paradise, the God who loves us gives the hope right back to us.

His earlier words to the serpent are words of condemnation for the evil one but words of a promise for us: "I will put enmity between you and the woman, and between your seed and her seed; he shall bruise your head, and you shall bruise his heel" (Gn 3:15).

We call this the *protevangelium*, the first Gospel. It is the great promise that, in the fullness of time, the serpent will be defeated. That will be put into motion by a woman's word, reversing the words of Eve: "May it be done to me according to your word" (Lk 1:38, NABRE).

Adjacent to the panels at the top of the Holy Door that depict the angel, Adam, and Eve are two more panels mirroring this fulfillment of God's promise: the angel Gabriel and Mary, the New Eve. We are propelled from the garden to the annunciation; from the angel who banishes to the angel who announces; from promise to fulfillment; from the loss of hope to hope restored.

The words we find here, stretching across these first panels, are not from scripture but from an ancient hymn praising Our Lady:

> What man hath lost in hapless Eve,
> Thy sacred womb to man restores.

The poem continues with the great announcement that now the weary mortals, sons of Adam, can enter the eternal doors of heaven.

So let us allow ourselves to be propelled into that next scene and find there the reason for our hope.

1

A Promise Fulfilled

There are many moments throughout time that could be said to have "changed history." History textbooks are written by connecting these moments together—battles and treaties, revolutions and movements, proclamations and decisions.

But the decisive moment that changed history forever was a battle won with a single sentence, a revolution begun by a simple proclamation. Through a young woman's "yes," the hope of the world became a reality.

Look with Hope

Let's first consider this scene visually, looking at the two panels of the Holy Door that depict the annunciation. Take some time with them, carefully considering all the details. What details strike you?

The plant next to the Blessed Mother calls to mind the sprout that was promised from the dead shoot of Jesse. The word found above it, *germine*, reminds us of "germinate." The trees and life outside Mary's window remind us of the hope of spring flowers coming forth from the seemingly dead winter ground.

It is traditional to depict the Blessed Mother with a book open near her during the annunciation. Despite the anachronism, it is a reminder to us that Mary knew the Hebrew Scriptures—the Law and the prophets—and she kept these in her heart. It is also a reminder to us that upon her consent to the angel's invitation, she becomes pregnant with the incarnate Word of God.

What do you see behind the angel Gabriel? Do these panels remind you of the panels of the Holy Door we're using in this study of hope? If you were to create a series of panels for your own holy door, reminders and memories of times God nourished your hope, what scenes would you choose to depict?

Who else is witnessing this scene for us? Like the open book, it has become traditional to depict a cat at the annunciation. The reasons, however, are disputed. Because cats are known for hunting mice and keeping vermin from the house, some say they are defenders against evil. At the same time, they are often associated with evil and are symbols in some religious art for Satan. Or maybe this little feline is just a touch of domestic normalcy in this otherwise earth-shattering event. What do you think?

Turn to the Word

Now let's turn to this same scene in the pages of the scriptures. As we begin this study of hope, I challenge you to read this story in Luke's gospel—even though it is perhaps quite familiar to you—as if you have never heard it before. This will require slowing down, reading each word carefully. Picture the scene as you read.

Imagine that you are a bystander, unnoticed by the young woman as she speaks with her heavenly visitor. What does she look like? How does her voice sound? What emotions can you hear or see?

This is the moment that changed human history forever. Take it in, slowly. This is the moment that changed our ability to hope.

✆ Read Luke 1:26–38

Before this moment, we had promises and prophecies. Hope was real, though it rested in the words of prophets and patriarchs. God came and dwelt with his people, yet remained at a distance—in an ark shadowed with a cloud, in a temple with a separation veil. God spoke, but through intermediaries.

At the moment of the annunciation, all that was changed forever. He came as one of us. Our hope had a name.

The promises to Abraham, Moses, and David had not been forgotten, despite what it may have felt like at times. God had promised these leaders that he would not forget his people. He had promised David that he would have an everlasting kingdom! When David wanted to build the Lord a house, the Lord turned the tables on him and promised to build David a house. In 2 Samuel 7, he made a big promise to David: to establish David's throne forever.

Looking at the history of the Chosen People, however, David's kingdom did not even last through the reign of his own grandson. In 931 BC, the northern tribes rebelled against King Rehoboam and the tribe of Judah. They made Jeroboam their king, splitting off as the kingdom of Israel. Over the next nine hundred years, the split kingdom suffered under captivity, exile, and occupation. The Davidic monarchy was never reestablished.

Did God forget his promise? Did he go back on his word? Psalm 89 gives voice to this question, as we see the author struggling with the tension between the promise of 2 Samuel and historical reality. The psalmist recalls that the Lord promised, "My merciful love I will keep for him for ever, and my covenant will stand firm for him. I will establish his line for ever and his throne as the days of the heavens" (Ps 89:29–30). But later in the psalm, he states, "You have renounced the covenant with your servant; you have defiled his crown in the dust. You have breached all his walls; you have laid his strongholds in ruins" (Ps 89:39–40). He asks, "Lord, where is your steadfast love of old, which by your faithfulness you swore to David?" (Ps 89:49).

What was it like to be one of the Chosen People at the time of the annunciation? Your people had been promised great things, and yet you now live under Roman occupation. Herod the Great ruled this area as a king, but his rule and "kingdom" were quite different from what had been promised to David. Herod was not only not of the house of David, he was an Edomite. A friend of Marc Antony, Herod became king not because of any Jewish lineage but by appointment of the Roman Senate.

It had to be tempting to throw one's hands up and say, "Hey, God? What's up with this?"

Recall the plant growing near Mary in our Holy Door panel. In the midst of the darkness, when the line of David appeared to be finished, the branch sprouts from a seemingly dead stump. In the annunciation, God reveals his plan: not to renege on his promises but to fulfill them in a much, much greater way than anyone had imagined.

Yet, at this moment, the fulfillment still remains shrouded in mystery. Remember, Mary is given very little information about what her "yes" will entail. She can't see the future, and Gabriel didn't exactly fill in all the details. What does she do next?

Pope Benedict XVI reflects, "The great hour of Mary's encounter with God's messenger—in which her whole life is changed—comes to an end, and she remains there alone, with the task that truly surpasses all human capacity. There are no angels standing around her. She must continue along the path that leads through many dark moments."[1]

We all have those moments of confusion over God's plan. Mary is an example of hope in the face of the unknown. She is asked to be open and obedient, and she trusts. The fulfillment of centuries of hope becomes flesh in her, but it does not mean she has all the answers. She must still walk forward in trust. And she does so in hope.

Respond with Faith

1. In Psalm 89, we see the psalmist wrestling with feeling abandoned by God, yet he ends with praise. Do you struggle to pray when you aren't "feeling" the words? How can you praise God even in times of darkness?

2. Can you remember a time when, in the moment, it felt like the Lord had broken his promises to you? In retrospect, in

what ways can you see God's hand, answering your prayers in a "bigger way"?

3. How have you been asked to trust in the Lord's plan without knowing all the details?

2

He Leads, We Follow

Have you ever been tempted to ask "so what?" when reading scripture stories? Sometimes we can hear these very familiar stories and wonder how they really affect us today. Or perhaps we can see more clearly how the world is suffering the effects of the Fall in the garden than how we're flourishing from the effects of the annunciation.

But Christ came to open the garden back up to us, and that doesn't just start after we die. If we are willing to follow him, that garden living starts now.

Look with Hope

Let's first consider this scene visually by looking at the panel that depicts the baptism of Jesus. Look at all the details of this scene. What captures your attention?

Notice the posture of Christ. His head is bowed, and his arms are crossed in humility and receptivity. Merely looking at this image, one would assume that John was the more important and powerful of the two men. The Latin inscription—*You come to me?*—voices John's protestation at this very role reversal.

To the left, we see an angel at the ready with a baptismal garment. Rather than an actual commentary on what happened at the baptism, this is intended to draw us into the scene to recall our own baptism. The words God the Father uttered over his beloved are applied to us, when we share in his baptism and thus in his divine sonship. Ponder that great mystery: you are called "child" by God!

Behind the angel we see a palm tree, a prevalent ancient symbol in Christian art to express triumph and victory over death. How can we share in the victory won by Christ's death and Resurrection? In the words of St. Paul, "We were buried therefore with him by baptism into death, so that as Christ was raised from the dead by the glory of the Father, we too might walk in newness of life" (Rom 6:4).

Turn to the Word

Now let's turn to this same scene in the pages of the scriptures. We will be reading Matthew's account of the baptism. Imagine that you are there that day by the Jordan, and you watch this event unfold. What do you see? What do you hear? Picture the scene as you read.

✺ Read Matthew 3:13–17

Before Jesus launches into his public ministry, he comes to the Jordan River to be baptized. We can't take this act for granted. What is he doing? John recognizes that Jesus is not in need of Baptism. He tries to prevent him, Matthew says, recognizing that the roles should be reversed. After all, the purpose of being baptized by John is repentance. The people had come to seek forgiveness for their sins, and they had been baptized by John as an outward sign of change and conversion.

And yet, Jesus, the last one who needs this, convinces John: "Let it be so now; for thus it is fitting for us to fulfil all righteousness" (Mt 3:15). There's that word again from the last scene we examined: *fulfill*. The promises had been made as early as the third chapter of Genesis. The plan was in motion. Jesus asks John to trust.

Jesus lowers himself to be numbered among the sinners. He, in the words of St. Paul, became sin for our sake (see 2 Corinthians 5:21). He stands in a line with those in need of conversion—the cheaters, the liars, the gossipers, the adulterers, the people who haven't darkened the door of a synagogue in years—he stands with them.

These are the ones he has come to save.

When Jesus enters the waters of baptism, he enters to show that he loves us, that he has come to be one with us, and that baptism is our way to salvation.

When he enters the waters, he sanctifies them. In the Sacrament of Baptism, it is the water that sanctifies us. But here, the waters don't cleanse the Son; he needs no cleansing. He goes into the waters to sanctify the waters. And in doing so, he shows us what are to do. He leads the way to hope. We too are to go into the water, to be plunged into the depths only to rise up into new life. We are buried so that we might rise.

Jesus has come to die for us, yes, but his gift does not end there. If he just came to die and rise again, how would we have access to that action two thousand years later? Jesus has come to give us access to this new life: grace. He has come to restore us to what was lost in the garden. And he does that through the sacraments.

Our hope rests not only in the fact that he has opened the gates of heaven for us, a gift to be given later after our death. No, his life of grace is for the here and now. We have reason to hope now because through the sacraments, he gives us his very life. Through the sacraments, he shares his divine sonship with us. "See what love the Father has given us, that we should be called children of God; and so we are. . . . Beloved, we are God's children now" (1 Jn 3:1–2).

The words spoken by the Father at Jesus's baptism also echo over us at ours: *This is my beloved son, this is my beloved daughter.* The hope of the resurrection, the hope of eternal life, is given at the beginning of our Christian journey when we receive our new identity as children of God.

We have a God who does not desire to call us "creature" or "servant," both titles we deserve. Rather, he calls us one that we do not deserve: "child." If we follow Christ into the waters, we have reason for great hope. In the coming chapters, we will explore further where following him leads.

Respond with Faith

1. The word *baptism* comes from the Greek word meaning "to plunge." The *Catechism of the Catholic Church* says, "The 'plunge' into the water symbolizes the catechumen's burial into Christ's death, from which he rises up by resurrection with him, as 'a new creature'" (*CCC* 1214). While water can be a source of life, it can also be a cause of death. How do each of these effects of water relate to baptism?

2. What does it mean to live as a child of God?

3. Why do you think Pope Francis encourages us to celebrate our baptismal anniversaries?

3

What Really Binds Us

I f Jesus walked into this room right now, what would you ask him to do in your life?

This was a question the people of Capernaum may have asked themselves. The miracle worker lived among them. What did they want from him? For a certain group of friends, we know exactly what they wanted: healing for their paralyzed friend.

Look with Hope

Let's first consider this scene visually, looking at the panel of the Holy Door that depicts the cure of the paralytic. Take some time with it, carefully taking in the details.

We see that the paralytic is naked yet partially covered, reminiscent of Adam after the Fall. This man is a representative of all sons and daughters of Adam, suffering under the effects of sin and yearning for freedom and healing. Jesus, the New Adam, stands ready to give him the healing he needs the most: the forgiveness of his sins.

The paralytic is also seemingly wrapped in his bed linens, evoking images of a burial shroud. As he reaches out to Christ, he reaches out to the One who will defeat death by his own death. Christ can save this paralytic from his current paralysis, but he has really come to save him from eternal death.

Interestingly, a prominent feature of this picture is the tiled roof above the two men. Both Mark and Luke mention his friends actually removing this roof to lower him to Jesus. Why might the artist have chosen to depict the roof and yet depict it intact? Is it to remind us that Christ has come to heal *all* the holes in our lives, many of which we ourselves have caused? What broken roofs do you need Christ to come fix?

Turn to the Word

Now let's turn to this same scene in the pages of the scriptures. Take your Bible and turn to the second chapter of Mark's gospel. As we have done with the previous stories, take time to read the passage, forgetting that you have heard it dozens of times before. Put yourself into the scene.

Perhaps imagine being in the crowd outside, trying to hear what Jesus is saying, and you see the friends coming up with their grand plan. Or maybe you are inside, and their plan comes to your attention as sunlight begins to stream into the room from a hole. Maybe you are the owner of the house, or a disciple, or one of the friends. Or maybe *you* are the paralytic.

ℰ *Read Mark 2:1–12*

In Mark's account, since the crowds were making it impossible to get to Jesus, the friends of the paralytic broke through the roof. I remember hearing this story as a child; the scene captured my imagination. Not knowing much about housing arrangements in the first century, I wondered what it was like to remove a roof. Was the owner angry?

There is something far more dramatic here, however, than a broken roof—or even a broken body.

The real story here is the cure of this man's soul. And thus, all of us can relate to the paralytic, regardless of our physical condition. All of us can find hope here.

Notice what Jesus first says to the paralytic: "Child, your sins are forgiven" (Mk 2:5). His first response to this man in need is not *your legs are healed*, but *your soul is healed*. His priority was the man's spiritual condition rather than his physical malady.

If we are going to understand how Jesus comes to save (and thus bring hope), we have to understand this priority.

Let us place ourselves in the position of the paralytic. What do you think he experienced when Jesus spoke those first words? Perhaps he felt confusion or disappointment. He had come to be physically healed; why was Jesus talking about sin? This physical paralysis was preventing him from living a free, full life. It was likely causing him anguish and suffering, perhaps both exteriorly and interiorly. He had come for a cure, and yet Jesus was speaking of *forgiveness.*

Are you struggling with the burden of a physical condition? Perhaps that is how you answered the question at the start of this chapter. You desire physical healing. Or perhaps your burden is something else: a relationship, financial difficulty, past trauma, or current addiction. All of us are carrying burdens that threaten our ability to live a full, free life. How can we have hope while we carry them?

The mystery of this encounter with the paralytic is that ultimately, Jesus has come to free us *not* from physical paralysis but from spiritual paralysis. Some of us will never know life without suffering. But that does not prevent us from hope. What Jesus offers is a freedom that is not impeded by earthly burdens.

Yes, the healings and cures performed by Christ throughout his public ministry are astonishing. This man picks up his mat to go home. The blind see. The lepers are cleansed. Even the dead are raised. But these physical cures are only signs and shadows of the real work Jesus is capable of doing: bringing the sons and daughters of Adam true freedom, joy, and peace—what they had longed for since leaving the garden.

It is not wrong to pray for healing or relief from the burdens you carry. But our hope lies not in a miracle worker come to give us relief or happiness but in a God come to save us from what really brings sadness and despair: distance from him.

Our sins separate us from our loving Father. Our mortal sins are choices we make to cut ourselves off from him fully, but even our venial sins build up barriers. The world tells us that freedom is the ability to do what we desire. If that is the case, why are there so many miserable "free" people? A life spent satisfying the desires of the flesh is truly unsatisfying, for those desires are insatiable. Far from freeing us, they enslave us, begging us to feed them more and more.

Freedom is the ability to do what we ought. It is the ability to choose to act in accordance with how and why we were made. As human persons, we were created not for sin but in the image and likeness of God.

This is the freedom Jesus came to bring. When he preaches in his hometown synagogue, he announces he has been sent "to proclaim release" and "liberty" to those held captive (Lk 4:18). This wasn't a release from physical bondage. It was a proclamation of a *spiritual Jubilee*, a spiritual release from what truly held people hostage.

If we are going to be people of hope, we must open our eyes to what truly causes despair. What paralyzes us is not our physical maladies or the heavy burdens we carry. It is our sins, which keep us from the only One who can transform those sufferings into joy.

No matter what burden you carry, hold fast to hope in the Lord, who is powerful enough to bring light in the darkness. And in future passages, we will find that no darkness is too dark, no sin is too great, nothing is beyond the scope of the Lord's forgiveness.

Respond with Faith

1. In the opening Turn to the Word, whom did you imagine yourself to be? Did this open up anything different or new for you in the story?

2. How can a physical suffering or burden separate us from Christ? How can it bring us closer to Christ?

3. What sin do you find yourself confessing most often? How do you see this sin paralyzing you in your daily life, in relationships, or in your work?

4

A Father's Heart

H ave you ever felt unworthy of God's mercy? The sin of despair can be present in our lives in different ways and to different degrees. At times, self-knowledge of our own weaknesses can lead us to wonder how God could love us. Repeating the same sins in the confessional (or perhaps a grave sin that haunts our past) can cause us to question if we're worthy to call ourselves a son or daughter of God.

Look with Hope

Once again, let's begin by looking at the Holy Door, taking in the details of the panel illustrating the scene of the prodigal son returning to his father. What details do you notice? Why do you think the artist chose these?

The father stands at the center of the scene, indicating to us that he, not the son, is the protagonist of this story (the title of the parable notwithstanding). While the two sons are important figures in the story, Jesus tells the parable to reveal something about the father, and our focus should be on him.

The son is barefoot, reminding us of his former position as a servant. While he's willing to remain in this role now that he's returned home, his father immediately shows he has other plans.

Who is sharing the joy of the father that the son has returned home? As with depictions of this scene by other artists, we see a little dog rejoicing at the homecoming. The dog is a traditional symbol of fidelity (hence the name Fido,) and reminds us of the faithfulness of the father's love despite the waywardness of the son—and us.

The setting of the scene at a well may indicate that the father has met the son while still far off from the house. But notice the other side of the rope is precariously loose. Are we witnesses of this scene, frozen in the instant before the bucket plummets into the deep well? This may indicate that the father, delirious in his sudden joy, has released the rope without thinking. Or perhaps it is an image of the depths of our heavenly Father's love and mercy for us.

Turn to the Word

With these images in our head, now let's turn to this same scene in the pages of the scriptures. Take up your Bible and find Luke's gospel. As we have done with the previous stories, take time to read the passage and imagine that you are hearing Jesus's voice tell this story for the first time. You are standing in a crowd, listening to him. There has been complaining and consternation about Jesus eating with tax collectors and sinners. In response to this discomfort and confusion, he tells this story.

✆ Read Luke 15:11–32

An entire Bible study could be written on this single parable. We will concentrate on one aspect: the radical mercy of the father toward his wayward son.

Let's begin by considering the son's speech of repentance, which we hear twice in the parable. He realizes he is no longer worthy to live in his father's house as a son. He has made his choice by taking his inheritance, essentially telling his father he didn't care about him.

This is what we do every time we sin. Sin is the decision to freely choose against God. Generally, we are choosing our own will over his. While we do this thinking it will make us happy, it ultimately leads to the opposite. Look at the son: he chose to leave the Father's house and squander his property. The word for *property* used here is *ousia*—the same word used in Greek philosophy for *essence*. He is not just spending his money on sinful things. In the process of doing so, he is squandering his very essence.

The son thought he would be free when he could do whatever he wanted, unburdened by the rules of his father's house. So he pursues pleasure, believing he will find happiness. And yet the road ends in a pigpen.

Swine are unclean according to Jewish law, and now he's surrounded by them. This son's quest for pleasure and freedom has led to slavery, life among pigs. Because, after all, he didn't just squander his inheritance. He was losing his identity.

As we saw in the last chapter, freedom is not found in doing whatever we please. It is found in living for God. And so how does Jesus describe his moment of realization and conversion? Some translations say he came "to his senses" but others say "he came to himself" (Lk 15:17). He remembers who he is. He remembers his identity as a son.

In his sin, he had forgotten who he was. He had forgotten he was truly loved by his father. He had forgotten what life was really about. Yet when he finally remembers, he judges himself unworthy to return to that state. His heart condemns him. He returns home, ready to be his father's servant. He rehearses his speech and is ready to accept what is rightfully his.

But the father's love and mercy are radical. When he sees his son from afar, indicating that he was watching for him, he embraces him before the son can even begin his rehearsed speech. And he does not let his son finish. Look at verse 21 as opposed to verse 18. The father does not even let the son ask to live as a servant.

On the contrary, he gives him a ring, a symbol of authority. Household slaves would normally be barefoot, but the son is given shoes. Neither son believes this is what the prodigal son deserves. It is a radical, undeserving show of mercy.

Perhaps we can relate to this feeling: knowing we do not deserve our Father's forgiveness. Our heart condemns us, and we are tempted to despair. There is a prayer in the Maronite liturgy on the Sunday of Lent that focuses on this parable: "Though my heart now condemns me, you are greater than my heart" (see 1 John 3:20).

That is the mystery of the boundless mercy of God, which gives us hope even after we choose to squander our essence. Our Father is greater than our hearts, which want to accuse and despair. He is ready to forgive.

Notice that the father never condones the actions of the son. Rather, he describes his son as being "dead" and now "alive." He recognizes that his son chose against his own nature, chose slavery over freedom. He acknowledges that he has sinned, but he welcomes his repentant son home. In mercy, he offers him the sonship he does not deserve.

That is how we can hope in the face of our own sin. Even when our own hearts condemn us, we can hope in the Father's mercy, if we fall at his feet and desire to reform ourselves. The divine sonship given at Baptism is not erased; nothing we can do removes that indelible mark on our souls given at Baptism.

God does not want us in the pigpen. At times it might be hard to come home, but when we come to our senses, our Father is not only waiting for us but ready to clothe us once again with the privileges of divine sonship.

Respond with Faith

1. What are ways we can increase our faith in the Father's love and mercy for us, even in the face of our knowledge of our weaknesses?

2. Why might it be hard to "come home" to the Father's house?

3. How might God be asking you to resemble the father? If there is someone in your life whom you are reluctant to forgive, are you imitating the father or the older brother?

5

The Necessity of Love

In our last scene, we met two sons: the younger son, who left home to live a sinful life, and the older one, who begrudged his father's clemency. Perhaps the older son presumed that he himself didn't need forgiveness. Or maybe he thought his little brother was presuming upon their father's mercy.

This older son is not unlike Simon the Pharisee, whom we meet in Luke's gospel when he invites Jesus over for dinner. As we'll see, Simon is horrified by what transpires when a sinful woman crashes the party to show her love for Jesus.

Look with Hope

Let's first consider this scene visually, examining the panel that shows us the woman anointing Jesus's feet. Look at all the details of this scene. What captures your attention?

The banquet table, strangely empty, separates the groups. Opposite Jesus is Simon, who sits in judgment or with great concern, and a man who seems completely disengaged and unaware of the scene.

Which side of the table am I on? What is my response to Christ?

On the shelf above Jesus is a series of dishes and what appears to be a mortar and pestle, an ancient tool for grinding spices. This tool tears seeds apart but, in doing so, releases oils that otherwise remain trapped inside, thereby causing wonderful aromas and flavors. This is an image of the penance we do for our sins. While penance is often painful, the grinding and discomfort not only strips away but also releases and transforms.

Jesus's hands are raised in both welcome and blessing. He allows the woman to do the work she has come to do, but he is immediately ready to embrace her with the loving arms of a merciful Savior.

Turn to the Word

Now let's turn to this same scene in the pages of the scriptures. As you have in the past, put yourself in the place of someone in the story. Maybe you are Simon, who has invited Jesus over for dinner. Maybe you are a fellow dinner guest, simply observing the scene. Or maybe you are the woman who has come seeking Jesus. What do you see? What do you hear? How do you feel?

ℰ Read Luke 7:36–50

Two distinct characters emerge in both the account of the dinner and Jesus's parable: Simon, the Pharisee who has invited Jesus over for dinner, and the sinful woman who comes uninvited.

Why has Simon invited Jesus? Luke doesn't tell us, but we can make several guesses. Perhaps he is curious to see who Jesus is. That seems to be indicated by his immediate conclusion at Jesus's reaction to the woman: "If this man were a prophet . . ." (Lk 7:39). Or perhaps he wants to show off his status by inviting the town's latest celebrity to his house.

Regardless, it is apparent Simon did not invite Jesus over to his house because he loved him. If he did love him, he would have at least shown him the basic courtesies of the time. And this is the crux of our story.

We have been looking at the boundless scope of God's mercy, which enables us to have the virtue of hope even in the face of our sins. But there is a sin against the virtue of hope called *presumption*. The person who commits the sin of presumption either believes he does not need God's help to be saved or he takes for granted God's mercy and believes he will be saved regardless of whether he is repentant or tries to change his ways.

In this scene, the penitent woman shows us the key to having hope without falling into presumption: love. She does not presume upon the Lord's mercy. Rather, in her actions, we see her love through her sorrow, humility, and penitence.

We can at times misunderstand the need to do penance. Is it because God likes to see me suffer? Is it because the Catholic Church likes to make people feel guilty? This woman shows us that penance must always be rooted in love. It is not about obeying a command by a God who delights in our suffering. It is about showing love to a God we are sorry for having hurt.

The woman knows she is a sinner and comes to Jesus in humility, washing his feet with her tears and drying them with her hair. She knows she needs God, she is sorry for having offended him, and she endeavors to show her love for him.

A clear juxtaposition to this attitude is Simon, who in his self-absorption does not even see his need for repentance. He shows by his actions that he has no love in his heart for Jesus, and therefore falls into the sin of presumption. He might call to mind another Pharisee in the Gospel of Luke, the one in Jesus's parable of the tax collector and the Pharisee going up to the Temple to pray (see Luke 18:9–14). Jesus tells this parable to "some who trusted in themselves that they were righteous": the definition of presumption.

Love is necessary for hope. First, God's love for us generates our ability to hope. Despite our sin, we know he loves us and we do not despair. Second, our love for God prevents us from falling into presumption. It allows us to see our sin for what it is. Knowing we have sinned against God who loves us, and striving to love him in return, we come to him in humility. We do penance out of love for him, anxious to do anything to show our sorrow and desirous to rid ourselves of anything that keeps us from him.

The lesson of this scene is not that we need to go out and commit great sins and then repent in order to be loved by God! St. Thérèse of Lisieux wrote that she was drawn to imitate the "loving audacity" of this woman, not because she herself had committed great sins, but because the only reason she *hadn't* committed them was due to the Lord: "Jesus has forgiven me more . . . since He forgave me in advance by preventing me from falling."[2]

It might be difficult to find a saint who is less like the penitent woman in terms of past sins—one of Thérèse's spiritual directors told her he didn't think she had ever committed a mortal sin.[3] And yet Thérèse attributed this to God's love for her and felt a kinship with this woman who loved so deeply.

Regardless of our past, we owe everything to the Lord, and we come to him in love. If we do, we too will hear the voice of the Lord saying, "Your faith has saved you; go in peace" (Lk 7:50).

Respond with Faith

1. St. Ambrose writes, "It was not the ointment that the Lord loved, but the affection; it was the woman's faith that pleased him, her humility. And you also, if you desire grace, increase your love; pour over the body of Jesus Christ your faith in the Resurrection, the perfume of the holy Church and the ointment of charity towards others."[4] In light of this, what is something you can do this week to show the Lord you love him?

2. You receive Jesus as a guest every time you receive Holy Communion. How can you welcome him as the penitent woman did and not as Simon did?

3. Have you been grateful for the Lord's forgiveness, or have you taken it for granted?

6

The High Cost of Mercy

F orgive us our trespasses as we forgive those who tres-
pass against us" (Mt 6:12). We say this line every time
we pray the Our Father, but do we really mean it?

What if someone hurts us again and again? Surely then we
are allowed to withhold forgiveness, right? Peter asked Jesus
this very question. Let's see what he says.

Look with Hope

Let's first consider this scene visually. A panel on the Holy
Door shows Peter coming to Jesus, asking a difficult question:
"Lord, how often shall my brother sin against me, and I forgive
him? As many as seven times?" (Mt 18:21–22). Look at the
panel carefully, taking in the various details.

Perhaps the first thing we see is the answer to the question
in Latin across the top of the panel. Maybe our heart sinks a
little as we read it: *seventy times seven*. A simple phrase. A
difficult answer.

The curtain behind Peter is reminiscent of the secrecy of
the confessional. The Lord waits for us in this place of great
mercy, ready to forgive us. He does so again and again. Am I
just as willing to forgive those who sin against me?

Why do you think the artist chose to include the bowl?
Maybe it is one of the bowls of God's wrath ready to be poured
out in Revelation 16. Jesus tells us how to avoid this wrath:
"Judge not, and you will not be judged; condemn not, and you
will not be condemned; forgive, and you will be forgiven" (Lk
6:37). Those are words that should give us great hope.

The door is cleaned between Jubilee years, but a patina forms in the years between restorations. Certain parts of the door remain shiny, as the countless hands of pilgrims touch parts of the panels. Christ's raised hand usually shines brightly, and this too has something valuable for us. Imagine yourself reaching out and touching the hand of Christ. The forgiveness he asks us to extend is only possible with him.

Turn to the Word

As you prepare to read this passage, place yourself in Peter's position and try to hear Jesus's words for the first time. You have come to Jesus with a good question, perhaps prompted by a personal experience. Someone has hurt you, and you know you need to forgive. But what if this is the second or third time this person has done this? Coming to the Lord, you likely feel you are being rather generous. *Seven times?*

I think we can all agree that that is remarkably patient. And yet, Jesus has an unsettling answer: "I do not say to you seven times, but seventy times seven" (Mt 18:22).

Jesus is using this expression not to suggest that Peter didn't have to forgive the 491st time, but to indicate that he needed to offer forgiveness without bounds or limits. Then Jesus presents a parable to drive the point home. As you read the parable, imagine how you would have responded had you been Peter.

❦ Read Matthew 18:21–35

The first servant owed the king a vast amount of money. The Greek literally reads "a myriad of talents," which translates to ten thousand talents. A *talent* was a measure of weight, so its worth would vary depending on whether it was made of gold, silver, or some other metal. But it is estimated that one talent could be up to twenty years of wages.[5] This man owes two hundred thousand years of wages!

Jesus is clearly making a point. The servant has borrowed more than he could *ever* repay. And yet the king forgives him.

The second servant owes a hundred denarii, which is about a hundred days' wages. While this is not a small sum, it is definitely repayable. The difference between the two debts is so radical and extreme that it is impossible to miss the Lord's point.

Who is the "wicked servant" of the parable? As we placed ourselves in the position of Peter, we should have felt a little discomfort while hearing Jesus's story. When we fail to forgive our brothers and sisters, even the fifth and sixth and seventh time they hurt us, we are the wicked servant.

Looking at the panel of the Holy Door, we can see Peter depicted coming to Jesus with his question. But we can also see it as the king and the servant.

When someone sins against us, it is nothing compared to how often and how greatly we have offended God. We can never repay our debt. He knows that, so he has paid it.

That is our reason for hope.

But this panel on the door reminds us that the hope comes with a price because mercy comes with a price. God wants to forgive our debts. He wants to free us from the shackles of sin. But it requires that we show others mercy.

The *Catechism* cautions, "Now—and this is daunting—this outpouring of mercy cannot penetrate our hearts as long as we have not forgiven those who have trespassed against us. . . . In refusing to forgive our brothers and sisters, our hearts are closed and their hardness makes them impervious to the Father's merciful love; but in confessing our sins, our hearts are opened to his grace" (*CCC* 2840).

It's not easy. As C. S. Lewis quipped, "Forgiveness is a lovely idea—until you have something to forgive."[6] But it's also important to remember that forgiveness is not a feeling. It's a choice. Even if you don't *feel* forgiveness toward someone, make the act of the will to forgive.

This does not condone the behavior of those who hurt us. Just as Christ's mercy is not a carte blanche for us to sin, forgiving others isn't giving them permission to hurt us again. But we have to make an act of the will to forgive them, even if they don't deserve it.

Hope comes at a cost: we must forgive others.

In our next passage, Peter will be dramatically placed in this parable, facing the King against whom he has sinned. But it's not just Peter. It is me too. I have sinned against the King, and yet I desperately want the hope and mercy that he has come to offer. Am I then willing to extend it to others?

Respond with Faith

1. What are some reasons it is so difficult to forgive?

2. Has there been a time in your life when receiving mercy changed or affected your understanding of mercy?

3. If there are people in your life you need to forgive, how can you begin the process even if you don't feel it in your heart?

7

Hope in the Face of Sin

In the last chapter, we looked at the parable of the forgiving king and the unforgiving servant. What does it look like when Peter becomes the servant in need of forgiveness?

Look with Hope

Let's first consider this scene visually. The panel we are going to look at now bears one of the most poignant verses in the gospels: "The Lord turned and looked at Peter" (Lk 22:61). It depicts the moment after the cock crows and Peter confronts the reality of his sin. Take some time with this scene, carefully taking in the details.

Prominently featured in the panel is the rooster, who almost appears to be still crowing. Peter's promise to stay faithful didn't even last a single night. The rooster has become a symbol of St. Peter. What would it be like to have an image of a great personal sin become a symbol for you?

The fire that Peter was warming himself by is small, almost unnoticed in the panel. This reminds us that the fire of Peter's passion and love, which had burned so brightly at the Last Supper, has burned down to mere embers.

There is a woman in the background who seems to stand between Jesus and Peter. Could this be Mary? Think of how Our Lady models for us what it is to accompany Jesus during the Passion: with love, fidelity, and strength drawn from prayer.

Turn to the Word

Now let's turn to this same scene in the pages of the scriptures. While this story is in all of the gospels, we will take our cue from the passage on the panel and look at Luke's account. As you read this familiar story, once again try to experience it as Peter did.

✎ Read Luke 22:31–34, 55–62

We can rationalize why Peter did what he did. We can feel with him the terror of being arrested, the discomfort of being ridiculed, the anxiety of the unknown, the confusion over what is happening to the man he had faith was the Messiah.

But we have to face that Peter abandoned his friend when he needed him most. And we must admit that not only do we follow this example of Peter, we profess belief in a Church whose other members and leaders do as well.

It can be easy for me to lose hope in Christ because of the sins of his ministers. We all know people who have left the Church because they or someone they know has been hurt by a member of the Church. Perhaps *you* have left.

But we only have to turn to the gospels to see that scandal, leadership failure, and sin have been with us since the Church's founding. Right after Jesus gives Peter the keys, he becomes a stumbling block for Jesus (Mt 16:22–23). And on this pivotal night, Peter denies that he even knows his Lord.

Don't you think that's something the gospel writers should have whitewashed? It shoots serious holes in your credibility to keep bringing up the fact that your first pope messed up . . . again and again and again. But this is the Good News of Jesus Christ: that he gave us a Church, not made up of sinless people, but made up of sinners (even the pope!). And the Church's goal is to make them into saints.

Jesus chose some seriously flawed men to be his first bishops. Read the gospels and list the character traits you see in those men prior to the crucifixion. Hot-headed, dense, cowardly, jealous. These were the first bishops. If I am honest with myself, I share some of those character traits.

The liturgy for Holy Thursday evening is one of my favorites of the liturgical year. The first part of the liturgy is a respite from Lent. We get to sing the Gloria, the priests and deacons are in white or gold vestments, and the altar is decked out in flowers. If you didn't know what happens next in the story, this chapter is pretty uplifting. Jesus lovingly washes his disciples' feet, and we get the gift of the Eucharist and the priesthood. What could go wrong?

But we do know the next chapter. And it hangs over the liturgy and its silent conclusion. After Mass, it is customary for the Eucharist to be brought to an altar of repose and for people to remain in adoration. We keep watch in the garden.

There, that night, Jesus needed his bishops the most. He had chosen these men as friends, confidants, literal *companions*, ones with whom he broke bread. And they abandoned him.

The day we celebrate the institution of the priesthood is the day we remember that the first priests were all failures hours later.

We are faced with the difficult reality that Jesus chose to institute a visible Church, one that is made up of flawed human beings. He chose to work through sons and daughters of Adam and Eve: bishops, priests, and you and me.

When these members of the visible Church disappoint, hurt, and abandon us, we have to remember that we are not alone. I am with Jesus, being abandoned by those who were supposed to stand by my side.

But this panel is a sign of hope in the face of that reality.

Right after Peter denied his friend and master three times, just hours after he solemnly swore he would never leave his side, that friend turned and looked at him. Think again of that sentence on this panel: "And the Lord turned and looked at Peter."

One can just imagine Peter recounting the story to Luke for his gospel. Could he ever forget that moment? The emotions he could still feel as he remembered the night, recalled that look—the simultaneous pain and love in Christ's eyes, the wordless exchange between Peter and his King.

He encountered the mercy of God that night. And he accepted the mercy.

Because I have to admit that I am Peter too. I abandon Jesus when he needs me most. And he is looking at me in mercy, as the merciful Father, the forgiving King. Am I willing to accept him?

In times of temptation to leave the Church or lose hope, we need to hold on to that figure that appears in the background of the panel. Our Lady is the perfect image of the Church. While we generally think of the Petrine dimension of the Church, the institutional hierarchy, there is also the Marian dimension of the Church. This isn't a division of the Church but an understanding of the various facets that make up the one diamond.

While our minds might first go to the visible Petrine dimension, Pope John Paul II speaks of this Marian dimension as being first and more fundamental and representative. This is because the Petrine dimension, in its functions of teaching and governing and administering the sacraments, has as its purpose to configure the Church, the People of God, into the ideal of holiness that Mary already is.[7] In times of darkness, whether because of our sins or the sins of others, let us cling to Mary and ask her to share her quiet strength and trust.

Respond with Faith

1. Trials, disappointments, and suffering can cause the fire of faith, hope, and love in our heart to die out. What are ways you can nurture the embers to keep them burning?

2. Why do you think Peter's denial is presented in all four gospels?

3. Who in your life has been a model of this Marian dimension of the Church: holy, faithful, trusting, full of hope?

8

Until the End

Y ou know when it's easy to have hope? On a sunny
day, when there's not a physical cloud in the sky nor
a metaphorical cloud on the horizon and everything
is going your way.

You know when it's hard to have hope? Hanging on a cross.

And yet we see the "good thief," whom tradition has named
Dismas, making one of the boldest declarations of hope in the
entire story of scripture. Let's look at that scene now.

Look with Hope

Once again, let's begin by looking at the Holy Door. Look at
the scene of the Crucifixion. What do you notice? What details
stand out to you?

If we look at the Latin inscription, we see that this depicts
a particular moment of that horrific afternoon. *Today you will
be with me in paradise.* It is the moment of salvation for that
man at Jesus's right hand.

Looking at Jesus's outstretched arms, we see that both
thieves are equidistant from him. Both are within his embrace.
Remember, the decision to turn to God or turn away from him
remains ours to make, and we are free to make that decision
until the very end. The thief at Jesus's left hand could have
repented and been welcomed into the kingdom too. He chose
otherwise, as we can tell from his bowed head. He turns away
from Jesus, his gaze down, thinking only of earthly realities.

Except for the halo and his crown of thorns, Jesus looks just
like the guilty. In his Incarnation, Jesus took on the limitations
of our humanity, and in his death, he took on the punishment

and sufferings we deserve for our sin. To bystanders that day, the innocent, spotless Lamb looked like a criminal.

Turn to the Word

With these images in our head, now let's turn to this same scene in the pages of the scriptures. Find Luke's gospel again. As we have done with the previous stories, take time to read the passage and imagine that you are witnessing these events for the first time.

✆ Read Luke 23:32–43

In some ways, Dismas and his counterpart remain a bit of a mystery to us. Legends have tried to fill in the gaps. How much did Dismas know of Jesus?

Jesus's response tells us all we need to know about Dismas. His request must have been made in faith, hope, and love of God, because it was enough for Jesus to grant him salvation.

Unlike the other thief, Dismas did not directly ask to be saved from their current situation. His request was for salvation, but not from the physical suffering they were enduring. He did not ask to be spared the cross; he simply asked the King to remember him. Did he understand the mystery of the kingdom to which he referred? Maybe not. But he spoke out in hope that despite his sin, Jesus could do something for him. He recognized that there was something more.

In the midst of this horrific suffering, he praised Jesus. He cried out to the bloody, weak man nailed to the cross next to him.

Think of the faith this required. It is easy to love God when life is comfortable. Praise comes effortlessly when blessings are easy to count. When we see God's goodness manifest itself in our lives through answered prayers, unforeseen profits, and happy events, it's not difficult to declare him King.

But we are called to be Dismas too. St. Gregory Nazianzen preached, "Worship him who was hung on the cross because of you, even if you are hanging there yourself."[8]

It must have been very difficult for Dismas to believe that the dying man hanging next to him was a king. But in the darkness, confusion, and pain, Dismas worshipped. He believed in the goodness of God, despite his present condition.

Dismas is a great reminder to us of hope. Despite our suffering, even if our cross seems too heavy, Jesus is still King.

Perhaps you wonder why you have this particular cross to carry. Maybe it is a cross you deserve, or perhaps it seems unjust. In the pain, it is tempting to complain, or worse, to follow the example of the other thief, who questions Jesus's power. In our suffering, it is easy to question the goodness of God. Does God love me? Is he all-powerful? If he could cure the leper and raise the dead, why can't he take away my cross?

Have the hope of Dismas. This suffering of this life will have an end, and then the gates of paradise await us.

Dismas is also an important reminder to us that, once again, no sin is too great for God's forgiveness. We are all in the middle of our stories, and it's not too late for anyone. We must have hope to the end: for ourselves and for our loved ones. Salvation is possible.

Cardinal Văn Thuận, a great model of hope himself, wrote while in prison: "The good thief achieved happiness because of his hope in the love of God; Judas was wretched because he despaired of this same love."[9]

Be Dismas.

Respond with Faith

1. Why are Judas and Dismas a worthy comparison for reflection?

2. When was a time in your life where you found it difficult to believe in God's goodness and power? What was your response in that suffering?

3. Why is it important to remember we are all in the middle of our stories? How can that help our interactions and relationships with others?

9

The Hope
of Being Found

There are so many obstacles to hope today, whether it's the crosses we carry, the shame of our own sins, or the pain caused by the sins of others. But we can struggle through these if we just know God is with us. What about hope in the face of his silence? How can we endure that?

Look with Hope

Study carefully the panel of the Holy Door portraying the Good Shepherd. Is this different from other depictions you have seen? What details stand out to you?

The scene is active and full of tension. The shepherd stretches out for a sheep that seems just beyond his reach. We find ourselves holding our breath, hoping his grip on the rock above him doesn't falter. The shepherd seems confident and in control, but this feat is not without effort. He goes to the extreme, to the end. And he does it for the disobedient sheep the world would tell him to forget.

The dog, again a symbol of faithfulness, guards a flock. Those are the faithful sheep who have not left the shepherd. In a surprising turn of events, it is he who has left them. What are we to make of this?

The Latin inscription is a reference to Jesus's words to repentant Zacchaeus in Luke 19:10: "The Son of man came to seek and to *save the lost*" (emphasis mine). There are various translations for *perierat*, including "lost," but it connotes much more than a wandering sheep; it is a perishing sheep.[10]

How will Jesus save that perishing sheep? How does he go searching for it? The form of his outstretched arms, reminiscent of the panel we just studied, gives us an indication of how that is to be accomplished.

Turn to the Word

As before, let's now open the scriptures. There are many passages depicting God as shepherd, and Jesus refers to himself as the Good Shepherd throughout the gospels. We will consider just one of these.

✆ Read Luke 15:1–7

This parable reminds us of an important aspect of God's mercy and love: He is not just a merciful father waiting for us to come home. He goes out looking for us. In his famous poem, Francis Thompson speaks of God as the "Hound of Heaven."

Whereas the shepherd was an established image of God in the Old Testament (see Ezekiel 34), there is an important uniqueness to Jesus as Good Shepherd. God the Father can feed and gather and protect and search for his sheep. But God the Son, after the Incarnation, can do something else: He can die for the sheep. "The good shepherd lays down his life for the sheep" (Jn 10:11).

Jesus is willing to go to the very deepest, darkest, farthest places for his sheep. He goes to Sheol.

In a statement that remains cloaked in mystery, we pray in the Creed that Jesus "was crucified, died and was buried; he descended into hell." Jesus willingly went to the farthest place he could to search for us. In an ancient homily for Holy Saturday, we hear, "What is happening? Today there is a great silence over the earth, a great silence, and stillness, a great silence because the King sleeps. . . . God has died in the flesh, and the underworld has trembled. Truly he goes to seek out our first parent like a lost sheep; he wishes to visit those who sit in darkness and in the shadow of death."[11]

What does it mean that God dies for me? Despite the frequency we speak or hear of this, we have to admit that if we really sit with it, it remains an uncomfortable mystery. God died.

In the Old Testament, there is one word for both *death* and *hell*: Sheol. It is utter aloneness, utter abandonment. On the Cross, Jesus cries out, "My God, my God, why have you forsaken me?" (Mt 27:46). Out of love for us, he embraces the worst thing we can possibly imagine: the darkness of feeling abandoned.

He descends into this hell, this Sheol of death and darkness and isolation. He has taken on every suffering of mankind imaginable, even this, the worst. In doing so, he destroys it. Because where Love himself enters, there is no longer isolation, abandonment, and loneliness.

Do you feel that God is absent? Does it seem that God is ignoring you? Perhaps you feel like yelling, "Hello, God? Remember me?!" Sure, Jesus told us to knock and the door will be opened. Sometimes I feel like I'm knocking and no one is home. People try to comfort me with nice words and pious phrases, but the temptation to despair deepens.

How can I have hope when God is silent? The words of the psalmist that became Jesus's now become mine. "My God, my God, why have you forsaken me? Why are you so far from helping me, from the words of my groaning? O my God, I cry by day, but you do not answer; and by night, but find no rest" (Ps 22:1–2).

Jesus has been there; he too has prayed those words. But this psalm ends in victory. Because when God was silent, when the King slept, he was accomplishing his greatest work. When he "rested" on Holy Saturday, he was saving the perishing sheep. Cling to that hope in the silence.

Maybe we are that lost little lamb in the panel. Or maybe we are part of the faithful flock that has not strayed. They too might look around and wonder where the shepherd has gone! Psalm 22 leads to Psalm 23. The Lord is our shepherd, and I have courage because I trust he is with me, even when silent (see Ps 23:4).

As Joseph Ratzinger wrote, "Where no voice can reach us any longer, there is he. Hell is thereby overcome, or, to be more accurate, death, which was previously hell, is hell no longer. Neither is the same any longer because there is life in the midst of death, because love dwells in it."[12]

Respond with Faith

1. Do you relate more to the little lone sheep or the faithful sheep in the flock? Or perhaps to both, at different times of your life?

2. If you only have hope when you feel God's presence or when God seems near, is that still hope?

3. What can you do in times when you *do* feel God's nearness
    to increase the virtue of hope to prepare for future days of
    suffering or dark nights?

10

Poured into Our Hearts

Is this life just a time of suffering until we are finally happy in heaven? At times it seems that all this talk about hope is just that: "Offer it up because heaven is worth it." Is it too much to hope for a little happiness here? Can God really transform my suffering into joy?

Look with Hope

As we try to wrap our minds around this mystery, let's look at the panel depicting Jesus's resurrection appearance to the disciples. Take some time with it, carefully taking in the details.

All eyes are fixed on him as they gather close. Can you imagine the transformation of the apostles' hearts from grief to joy upon seeing the Lord?

Jesus's hand is raised in blessing. While he rebukes the apostles for their lack of faith (see Mark 16:14), he ultimately comes to bring peace. How does he bring this peace? It's more than just a shocked relief that their friend is alive. The panel text reminds us of the gift he gives them that night: *Receive the Holy Spirit.*

Note that there are only ten apostles present, reminding us that Judas has abandoned the Lord. (We'll address Thomas's absence in the next chapter.) Despite his actions on Holy Thursday, Judas could have been here, in this room. Jesus was ready to forgive him. But Judas chose otherwise.

Turn to the Word

Now let's turn to this same scene in the pages of the scriptures. While every gospel account has various details of Jesus's post-Resurrection appearances, we will take our cue from the inscription on the panel and read from the Gospel of John.

ᕈ Read John 20:19–23

John the Evangelist seems to be the master of understatement in this passage: "Then the disciples were glad when they saw the Lord" (Jn 20:20). Their crucified friend stands among them . . . alive!

Think of the range of emotions in their hearts. Relief, astonishment, incredulity, joy, fear, embarrassment? After all, they had abandoned Jesus. And yet the first word he had for them was "peace."

Not only does he seem to forgive them, he speaks of *them* being able to forgive sins through the Holy Spirit! It is quite a night.

This gift of the Holy Spirit, an anticipation of what will occur on Pentecost, is the key to hope. Hope is impossible without him.

There is one apostle missing from this scene because of a sin against the Holy Spirit. We've already looked at one sin against hope, that of presumption. But the opposite side of the coin is the sin of despair. Man commits the sin of despair when he "ceases to hope for his personal salvation from God, for help attaining it or for the forgiveness of his sins" (*CCC* 2091). While Judas regrets his action, it seems that he despairs when he hangs himself instead of coming to Jesus for mercy. It is important to remember, however, since none of us can know the state of someone's soul when they meet God after death, we do not know the fate of Judas with certainty. We entrust him, as we entrust all the departed, to the mercy of God.

Jesus speaks of this failure of hope when he speaks of "blasphemy against the Spirit," which cannot be forgiven (Mt 12:31). It is not that God does not want to forgive every sin; rather, he cannot forgive someone who refuses to accept his mercy.

On Easter night, Jesus comes to bring hope and joy because he comes to bring the peace of the Holy Spirit. This peace is not a mere human emotion of elatedness or pleasure. It is something much deeper, something the world cannot understand.

When you are carrying a great cross or when the future looks bleak, you might wonder how the third person of the Trinity is going to help you. But we cannot forget that hope is a *gift*. When the world is closing in on you, when the pain is too much to bear, when you wonder why the Lord seems to trust you with crosses you cannot carry: turn to the Holy Spirit. He wants to activate in you his gifts of understanding, knowledge, wisdom, counsel, fortitude, piety, and fear of the Lord. These are what you need.

Only God can give you peace. And he can only give it now, in the present moment.

Despair occurs when we linger either in the past or in the future. Shame, regrets, and sins of the past make us question God's mercy. Uncertainty and anxiety about the future make us question his goodness.

But where is his grace? In the present moment. For God, there is no past and future. He is eternally present. This is why it's so dangerous to live in either the past or the future. Grace isn't present there. Does the past cause remorse? Go to Confession and embrace the graces of the present moment. Does the future frighten or worry you? Give your anxieties to the

Lord. When the future becomes the present, his grace will be present.

We are not called to live a miserable existence until heaven. We can have joy here on this earth, but it will not be happiness according to human standards. Rather, it will be the "peace of God, which passes all understanding." This can be found in striving to live in the present moment, entrusting everything to the Holy Spirit, who will "keep your hearts and your minds in Christ Jesus" (Phil 4:7).

There is great suffering in this life. But that is not all this life is destined to be. Is our hope ultimately for heaven? Yes. But God does not call us into a life of dreary existence, one day of suffering following the next. He calls us into a life of peace and joy. And in the next chapter, we'll see that he wants even our wounds to be transformed into glory.

Respond with Faith

1. How do you find yourself drawn out of the present moment in your daily life? How can you focus your attention and presence back to the present?

2. Bl. Solanus Casey said, "We must be faithful to the present moment or we will frustrate the plan of God for our lives."[13] How is God calling you to this faithfulness, especially in small, ordinary daily ways?

3. When have you experienced the "peace of God, which passes all understanding" (Phil 4:7)? How can that memory nourish your hope?

11

The Only Man-Made Thing in Heaven

Why was Thomas missing on Easter night? When he hears the report from the other ten apostles, he boldly declares, "Unless I see in his hands the print of the nails, and place my finger in the mark of the nails, and place my hand in his side, I will not believe" (Jn 20:25).

What was it that prompted this abrupt declaration? Are these perhaps the words of someone who has been so dejected and hurt by the events of the weekend that he vows never to be so vulnerable again? Jesus is prepared to enter into those feelings and transform them.

Look with Hope

Let's first consider this scene visually, looking at the panel of the Holy Door that depicts Thomas with Our Lord. Take some time with it, carefully taking in the details.

We see one of the other apostles peeking around a corner, perhaps indicating that Jesus came to Thomas for an intimate encounter, not a public "I told you so!"

The ellipsis in the phrase written across the top, *Blessed is the one . . . who has believed*, is included for a crucial reason: the words omitted—"who has not seen"—should be filled in by our memories. With those words, the phrase cannot be applied to either Thomas or that other apostle who peeks around the corner. After all, while Thomas has the bad reputation of being the "doubter," none of the apostles believed in the Resurrection until they saw it with their own eyes. We are called to be those whom the panel praises.

Jesus's wounds are visible, and he offers them to Thomas. This was what Thomas had demanded, and Jesus condescends to his request. He has a glorified body, but his wounds are still visible. Why?

Turn to the Word

Now let's turn to this same scene in the pages of the scriptures, continuing the passage we began reading in the last chapter. Put yourself into the scene. Maybe you are one of the apostles, anxiously waiting to see what happens when Thomas realizes you were telling the truth. Or maybe you are Thomas himself.

✆ Read John 20:24–29

Thomas needs to see Jesus's wounds. It's not just that he needs proof to believe in the Resurrection. Jesus wants him to see the scars of love.

Perhaps this is why Jesus appeared to the apostles without Thomas on Easter Sunday. Maybe he wanted Thomas's profound declaration of faith (the strongest statement of belief we've gotten from an apostle thus far) to be a revelation for those of us who struggle with our own wounds. It was in seeing and touching *wounds* that Thomas was moved from doubt to faith in the living God—a God who could work all things for good (see Romans 8:28).

The image that the apostles had of the Messiah had to die so that something greater could emerge.[14] Thomas now believes not just in a miracle worker or a great preacher but in a God who can transform the greatest evil (deicide) into the greatest good (salvation).

Christ has chosen to retain the nail marks in his flesh. Indeed, he has chosen for those marks to be an identifying factor of him for Thomas. Because they are marks of power.

We know very little about heaven and the glorified state; after all, none of us have been there. From the Resurrection appearances, however, we can gather certain things, including the fact that the resurrected body is a real, fleshly body (a ghost cannot eat) and yet has properties like the ability to pass through walls.

You would think that Jesus's resurrected body would be the body of perfect Adam, without flaw or imperfection. And yet there is something important about that resurrected body: it still bears the wounds of what Christ suffered.

We all have wounds. Some are bigger than others. Some are more public than others. Some are hard to hide, whereas some can be tucked neatly away so that the neighbors never know.

A moment in our childhood or a past relationship that has scarred us. A sin that makes us question whether God could still love us. A broken friendship; a grudge it's hard to let go of; verbal, physical, or sexual abuse. Those wounds play games in our head, telling us we'll never be good enough. We'll never be smart enough, capable enough, holy enough.

Jesus stands in front of you, his marked palms outstretched. He has wounds too.

And they are wounds of glory. They are wounds of hope.

Someone once said that the wounds of Christ are the only man-made thing in heaven. They are a reminder of sin, the price of our disobedience and self-love. But they have been transformed into marks of glory. Because they are not just what we did to our God. They are a reminder of what he did for us.

The all-powerful God can transform any wound, any sin, any cross into glory.

What does God want to do with your wounds? If we could travel back in time with a special machine that could eliminate every single moment of pain and suffering from our lives, would we honestly want that? Think of how your life today would be different. It's a mixed bag, is it not?

One of the great mysteries of love is that it is not possible without pain. Would we want to eliminate the experiences of love in our lives? We cannot grow in virtue without suffering and stretching. Would we want to go back to who we were before the lessons and perspective that suffering taught us?

There was an ancient belief that pearls were formed by the storms at sea. Despite the wounds that others have given us, or we have given ourselves, the mystery of suffering is that it also produces great pearls.

It is up to us to decide: Are those wounds going to stop us from loving, living, trusting, and hoping? Or are we going to allow God to work them for the good? Do we believe he has the power?

Joy will only come when we see his wounds—and ours—as signs of love and doorways of hope. In the last chapter, we will look at what this new perspective calls us to do.

Respond with Faith

1. How can your past experiences be obstacles to faith and hope?

2. What do you think of the statement that love is not possible without pain? Where have you seen this in your own life?

3. In his apostolic letter on the Christian meaning of suffering, Pope John Paul II speaks about the question that arises when we suffer: *Why?!* He says, "Christ does not answer directly, and he does not answer in the abstract this human questioning about the meaning of suffering. Man hears Christ's saving answer as he himself gradually becomes a sharer in the sufferings of Christ."[15] What do you think he means by this?

12

Go and Do Likewise

Throughout this study, we have looked at various reasons why we can have hope, no matter what our past or our future. We also must recognize that hope is a gift of God, and so while there are ways we can cultivate it and increase it, we ultimately have to begin by asking for it.

Now we must ask ourselves: As people of hope, what is our responsibility? Let's look at the story of a man who received a great gift from the Lord and consider what he did with it.

Look with Hope

Turn to the panel depicting the conversion of Paul. As we have done with the others, we'll begin by looking at this scene visually. Take some time with it, carefully studying the details.

Notice that this panel makes it clear that Paul encounters the glorified, resurrected person of Jesus. He doesn't just see a bright light or hear a voice. Paul meets the risen Lord, as Mary Magdalene and the disciples did. He thus becomes a witness of the Resurrection and is commissioned with the same responsibility they were.

The foliage that surrounds Paul reminds us of the panel depicting the garden. Adam and Eve left the garden, covering their eyes out of shame and sin (see page 3). Paul is about to encounter the gifts of the garden through the sacraments at the hands of Ananias, and his eyes will see again.

His horse's hoof is raised, reminding us that Paul was on a journey and a mission when Jesus intervened. Paul thought he knew his purpose; Jesus dramatically interrupted it to give him another.

Is there a building tucked up there, in the distance? Is it Damascus? Or does it bring our thoughts to Rome, where Paul will eventually be sent as a witness? (See Acts 23:11.)

Turn to the Word

Now let's turn to this same scene in the pages of the scriptures. This story occurs three times in the Acts of the Apostles: once when it happens to Paul (Acts 9) and twice when Paul recounts it to different audiences (Acts 22 and 26). We will read Paul's account of his conversion to a Jewish gathering in Acts 22. As we have done with the previous stories, take time to read the passage and put yourself into the scene, listening to Paul's story.

✑ Read Acts 22:1–16

Notice that when Paul tells his story, he emphasizes to this crowd that his conversion to Christ is not a rejection of his Jewish faith but a fulfillment of it. He uses this opportunity, as he will in Acts 26 in front of Festus and Agrippa, to preach the Gospel to the audience present.

If we were going to choose the perfect preacher of the Gospel, would we choose someone with Paul's history? Paul was responsible for the death and imprisonment of countless Christians. Couldn't God pick someone with less mess in his past? We see in Acts 9 that Ananias is a little afraid when he finds out he must go baptize Paul, and he even tries to argue with God! But God reminds us that his ways are not our ways (see Isaiah 55:8–9). He instructed Ananias, "Go, for he is a chosen instrument of mine to carry my name before the Gentiles and kings and the sons of Israel" (Acts 9:15).

It is Paul's past that equips him for the work (see 1 Tim 1:16). After having received mercy and been given true hope in Christ, he is sent out to witness and give hope to others. Throughout Acts, we see that an encounter with the risen Christ leads to a responsibility to give witness (see Acts 1:8, 21–22; 2:32; 3:15; 5:32; 10:39; 13:31). Paul recounts that Jesus gives him this same mission, through Ananias: "For you will be a witness for him to all men of what you have seen and heard" (Acts 22:15). As his eyes were opened, he will now go to others so that they may have their eyes opened (see Acts 26:16–18).

We are called to do the same as Paul. First, Paul recognizes that this mercy is a gift from God. "Last of all, as to one untimely born, he appeared also to me. For I am the least of the apostles, unfit to be called an apostle, because I persecuted the Church of God. But by the grace of God I am what I am, and his grace toward me was not in vain" (1 Cor 15:8–10).

Secondly, he gives thanks to God for it. "I thank him who has given me strength for this, Christ Jesus our Lord, because he judged me faithful by appointing me to his service, though I formerly blasphemed and persecuted and insulted him; but I received mercy because I had acted ignorantly in unbelief, and the grace of our Lord overflowed for me with the faith and love that are in Christ Jesus" (1 Tim 1:12–14).

Thirdly, he goes out to witness and share that gift with others. "Of this gospel I was made a minister according to the gift of God's grace which was given me by the working of his power. To me, though I am the very least of all the saints, this grace was given, to preach to the Gentiles the unsearchable riches of Christ, and to make all men see what is the plan of the mystery hidden for ages" (Eph 3:7–9).

He continues to preach hope in God's goodness and mercy even as he suffers for the Gospel (see 1 Timothy 4:10 and Ephesians 2:12–13). As we discussed previously, Paul recognizes that through the gifts of the Holy Spirit, active in his life, he can have hope and even joy despite the interior and exterior suffering he endures. "We rejoice in our sufferings, knowing that suffering produces endurance, and endurance produces character, and character produces hope, and hope does not disappoint us, because God's love has been poured into our hearts through the Holy Spirit who has been given to us" (Rom 5:3–5).

This is our mission as well. As people of hope, we must be preachers of hope. It is not enough to receive the gift of hope; rather, we now must share it with others. Our pasts don't prevent us from being instruments of hope—they equip and command us to be.

Respond with Faith

1. How has your past equipped you to share the Gospel, even in ways you might not expect, like Paul?

2. What can you do to better recognize and thank God for the gifts of mercy and hope?

3. Who is someone in your life that needs to hear the Gospel of hope?

STO · AD · OSTIVM
ET · PVLSO

CONCLUSION

Moving Forward in Hope

As we look at this last panel of the Holy Door, we recognize that this one is not like the others. Or is it? Rather than a story from scripture, we have a depiction of Pope Pius XII opening the Holy Door in 1949 for the Jubilee year. And yet this panel, just like the others, tells the story of hope.

In this final panel, we see that this story we've been praying with has been our story the entire time. Not just a story to study or passages from history, it is a story to live.

This final panel is an invitation into the story. As the first panels depicted the door of paradise being closed on our parents, this last panel shows that the door is open for us to walk forward in hope.

This is not simply a door in a church for pilgrims to Rome. It is a threshold for all of us on the pilgrimage of life, choosing to walk forward with hope in Christ, even when we cannot see the Resurrection through the darkness of suffering today.

The choice is ours. The words across the top of the panel quote Jesus in the third chapter of Revelation: "Behold, I stand at the door and knock" (Rev 3:20). While he has opened the gates for us, the choice is still ours. Will we open the door of our hearts to him?

Go Forward in Love

1. Hope is a gift. Find or write a short act of hope and incorporate it into your daily prayers. Pray it when you feel overwhelmed with shame about the past or worry about the present.

2. Paul tells us, "Rejoice in your hope, be patient in tribulation, be constant in prayer" (Rom 12:12). Commit to increasing your daily conversations with God. How can you receive the sacraments more often? Hope is only possible with him.

3. When your conversations with family or friends veer toward complaining, anxiety, or worry, choose instead to be a beacon of hope.

Notes

1. Pope Benedict XVI, *Jesus of Nazareth: The Infancy Narratives* (New York: Image, 2012), 37.

2. Thérèse of Lisieux, *Story of a Soul: The Autobiography of St. Thérèse of Lisieux* (Washington, DC: ICS Publications, 1996), 83.

3. Thérèse of Lisieux, *Story of a Soul*, 149.

4. St. Ambrose, in *The Navarre Bible: Saint Luke's Gospel*, 3rd ed. (New York: Scepter Publishers, 2005), 87.

5. Curtis Mitch, "Introduction to the Gospels," in *The Ignatius Catholic Study Bible: The New Testament* (San Francisco: Ignatius Press, 2010), 39.

6. C. S. Lewis, *Mere Christianity* (New York: Macmillan, 1977), 104.

7. John Paul II, "Discorso di giovanni paolo ii ai cardinali e ai prelati della curia romana ricevuti per la presentazione degli auguri natalizi," *L'Osservatore Romano*, December 22, 1987, https://www.vatican.va/content/john-paul-ii/it/speeches/1987/

december/documents/hf_jp-ii_spe_19871222_curia-romana.
html.

8. International Commission on English in the Liturgy, "Homily of Gregory Nazianzen," *Office of Readings* (New York: Catholic Book Publishing, 1976), 393.

9. Francis Xavier Nguyễn Văn Thuận, *The Road of Hope: A Gospel from Prison* (Boston, MA: Pauline Books & Media, 2001), 53.

10. In the original Greek, this word is the same as that used in John 3:16, "For God so loved the world that he gave his only-begotten Son, that whoever believes in him should not *perish* but have eternal life" (emphasis mine). See also Matthew 18:14.

11. "The Lord's Descent into Hell," ancient homily for Holy Saturday, https://www.vatican.va/spirit/documents/spirit_2001 0414_omelia-sabato-santo_en.html.

12. Joseph Ratzinger, *Introduction to Christianity*, rev. ed., trans. J. R. Foster (San Francisco: Ignatius Press, 2004), 301.

13. Tom Hoopes, "Fully American, Fully Catholic: Blessed Solanus Casey and St. Elizabeth Ann Seton," Seton Shrine, July 29, 2023, https://setonshrine.org/fully-american-fully-catholic -blessed-solanus-casey-and-st-elizabeth-ann-seton.

14. Ratzinger, *Introduction to Christianity*, 295.

15. John Paul II, *Salvifici Doloris*, February 11, 1984, III. 26, https://www.vatican.va/content/john-paul-ii/en/apost_letters /1984/documents/hf_jp-ii_apl_11021984_salvifici-doloris. html.

Joan Watson—a Catholic speaker, writer, and podcaster—is the associate editor of Integrated Catholic Life and the pilgrim formation manager for Verso Ministries.

Watson earned a bachelor's degree in history from Christendom College and a master's degree in theology and Christian ministry from Franciscan University of Steubenville. She has worked for the Church and various religious apostolates for more than fifteen years.

She is the founder of Living 1 John 1, an online community dedicated to helping Catholics pray and love scripture.

Watson lives in South Bend, Indiana.

joanwatson.faith
Facebook @joaninordinarytime
Instagram: @joan.m.watson
YouTube: @joanwatson
X: @joannie_watson

Greg Kandra was ordained as a deacon for the Diocese of Brooklyn in 2007 and most recently served as a senior writer at the Catholic Near East Welfare Association. He is the author of *A Deacon Prays* and *Befriending St. Joseph* and writes *The Deacon's Bench* blog.

AVE
AVE MARIA PRESS

Founded in 1865, Ave Maria Press,
a ministry of the Congregation of
Holy Cross, is a Catholic publishing
company that serves the spiritual and
formative needs of the Church and its
schools, institutions, and ministers;
Christian individuals and families; and
others seeking spiritual nourishment.

For a complete listing of titles from

Ave Maria Press

Sorin Books

Forest of Peace

Christian Classics

visit www.avemariapress.com

AVE MARIA PRESS
Notre Dame, IN
A Ministry of the United States Province of Holy Cross